ON THE ROAD TO FAME

Gustav Klimt was born on July 14, 1862 into a very poor family. He had two brothers, Georg and Ernst, and four sisters. His father was an engraver who drew decorative patterns on metal, but it was a job that barely brought in enough money to feed his family. Despite this, Gustav's father made sure that his three sons had a good artistic education. Georg became a metal sculptor, while Ernst and Gustav studied at art college.

They were very lucky to have grown up at a time when business was booming, not only in the capital city of Austria, Vienna, but in other, smaller towns as well. New buildings were going up everywhere, and lots of artists were needed to decorate the palatial townhouses of the new wealthy class — as well as stations, theaters, opera houses, museums, and university buildings — with rich designs and magnificent paintings. In Vienna, for example, work had been started on a grand new street called the "Ring."

Gustav, his brother Ernst, and an artist friend Franz Matsch, joined forces and founded their own artists' company. They soon became well known for their ceiling and wall paintings — or frescoes — showing scenes from the past, which they painted in a number of theaters throughout the monarchy.

After painting the auditorium in Vienna's "Burg Theater" with the most famous faces of the day, Gustav received a special award from Emperor Franz Joseph. It was called the Emperor's Prize and was worth 400 gold ducats. For months on end society ladies and gentlemen had queued up outside the artists' studio to have their portraits painted and be included in the fresco. Some of the women, however, who he had to turn away, couldn't hide their disappointment and are reported to have burst into tears.

GUSTAV KLIMT'S CEILING FRESCO FOR THE NEW BURG THEATER

JOSEF LEWINSKY, AN ACTOR AT THE THEATER

THE AUDITORIUM IN THE BURG THEATER

A PASSION FOR ANCIENT HISTORY

Gustav Klimt was greatly impressed by the art of the Greeks and Romans. When he was a student at art college and even later on, he liked to visit the "Imperial and Royal Museum of Art" to look at the vases and sculptures from that period, and to draw them. The new art form that he wanted to create was to be based on these ancient shapes and should have the same elegant lines. Again and again the Greek goddess Pallas Athena, who fought for justice and who stood for wisdom and the arts, can be seen in Gustav's paintings. Pallas Athena was to become the patron saint for this new art style. Gustav painted her wearing a golden helmet and protective armor plating.

Even in his portraits and other paintings, figures from the Classical period can be found. On the frame around one of his paintings, for instance, Gustav painted Apollo, the Greek god of music, with his lyre; and in a poster he designed for the first Secession exhibition he included several ideas taken from Ancient History.

4

PALLAS ATHENA

MEDICINE   PHILOSOPHY   JURISPRUDENCE

VIENNA AROUND 1900

The beginning of the twentieth century was an incredibly thrilling time. Many new inventions were beginning to bring a big change to people's everyday lives and habits: Electric lighting was now being used, messages could be sent by telegraph, and the telephone was soon to follow. The first automobiles could be seen on the streets as well as electric trams; the first cinemas opened their doors, and the first motorized planes took to the air. Underground railways were built; in Vienna it was known as the "city train." In Vienna, the famous doctor Sigmund Freud started to look more closely at the way we think and what we dream.

Artists responded to these changes with completely new and often baffling works of art. Architects started to build houses without any form of decoration; composers tried to create a totally new type of music; and painters no longer painted just what they could see but also what they thought.

Gustav Klimt, for example, was to create ceiling frescoes for the University of Vienna, showing the three faculties — philosophy, medicine, and jurisprudence. In his painting *Medicine*, however, Gustav didn't praise the latest achievements made in medical research, as the professors at the university had wanted, but, instead, he emphasized that we as humans can only partly govern the course of our lives and are powerless in the face of illness, pain, and death.

Gustav was viciously attacked for this, and was so insulted that he gave back the money he had been paid by the state and withdrew his three paintings.

HYGIEIA, DETAIL FROM MEDICINE

THE SECESSION BUILDING

Just before the end of the nineteenth century, in the year 1897 to be precise, a group of painters, draftsmen, sculptors, and architects founded the "Vienna Secession." Many had been members of the "Viennese Artists' House" but had been disappointed with it because the same things were always being repeated, and nothing new was ever attempted.

The members of the "Secession," on the other hand, wanted a completely new approach to art. And so a wonderful exhibition building was built (designed by the architect Joseph Maria Olbrich) that looks a bit like a Roman temple with a dome of gleaming golden laurel leaves on top. This was where not only member artists would show their latest works but also other interesting artists from all over the world. The people of Vienna came and marveled at Japanese woodcuts or the works of famous French, Dutch, British, and Scandinavian artists such as Claude Monet, Vincent van Gogh, Charles Rennie Mackintosh, and Edvard Munch.

LOOKING FOR A NEW ARTISTIC STYLE: THE SECESSION

At one of the exhibitions, a large sculpture of the composer Ludwig van Beethoven was shown. It was made by a German sculptor called Max Klinger, who was famous at that time, using brightly colored precious stones, bronze, and ivory. Gustav decorated the walls of the exhibition hall with a work that became known as the *Beethoven Frieze*.

The frieze includes a monster, nasty witches, and bad spirits — or "hostile powers" — that are a threat to human life, and virtually all the figures Gustav painted have no clothes on. The artist was convinced that love was stronger than any evil or danger, and so he finished off his wall painting with a picture of a man and woman hugging each other. The way Gustav painted the figures in his large fresco was, at that time, not considered to be decent, and his *Beethoven Frieze* started a real scandal.

THE HOSTILE POWERS
FROM THE BEETHOVEN FRIEZE

"HERE'S A KISS FOR ALL THE WORLD" FROM THE BEETHOVEN FRIEZE

SUMMER BREAKS

GUSTAV AND EMILIE ON LAKE ATTER

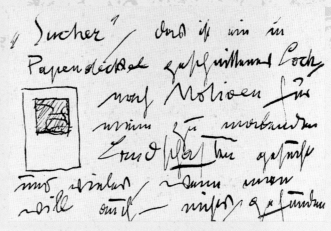

A LETTER WRITTEN BY GUSTAV IN WHICH HE SKETCHED HIS "VIEWFINDER"

Gustav spent many summer vacations in the countryside with Emilie, her sisters, and their mother. They usually went to Lake Atter in an area of Upper Austria called the "Salzkammergut." They spent their time paddling, swimming, playing tennis, hiking, cycling, or simply chatting, reading, writing letters, and taking gentle strolls. This type of long break away from city life was very fashionable at that time and often lasted several months. Some families used to take a lot of their own belongings with them and were accompanied by their staff. Gustav's canvases, brushes, paints, and his easel would arrive in big crates together with his other household things. And it was while he was on one of these summer vacations that he started to paint landscapes.

To find the best motif to paint Gustav made a "viewfinder." It was a small piece of cardboard with a square opening cut out in the middle. Over and over again, he used to look through his viewfinder to see what a tree, a house, or the water in the lake would look like on canvas. Apart from a few early attempts, all of his landscapes were, as a result, square-shaped.

Gustav's landscapes were to be carefully balanced pictures with a calm beauty of their own — as well as being a colorful feast for the eyes. He painted contrasting colors next to each other with great skill: red next to green, blue next to orange, yellow next to violet. He knew that this would make his pictures gleam and sparkle all the more. Gustav often only completed his paintings much later after he had returned to his studio in Vienna.

Gustav loved his summer breaks, but otherwise he didn't like leaving Vienna. However, when he did travel to cities such as Munich, Paris, London, or Madrid he felt homesick after just a few hours, and longed to be back home again. He also longed to see the girls and women of Vienna again, who he always found to be the most beautiful in the world.

A FARMHOUSE ON LAKE ATTER

GUSTAV'S LANDSCAPES

GUSTAV WITH A TELESCOPE

GUSTAV IN THE GARDEN OUTSIDE HIS STUDIO
IN VIENNA

Gustav Klimt didn't go far from his house to paint landscapes. He just went a few steps or even painted from the window or the terrace of the house where he was spending his vacation. Very carefully he picked out the details of the countryside or the buildings he could see in front of him. He always went to great lengths to make these into a colorful picture, covering his canvases with bright patterns like on a cheerful carpet.

Everything had to appear to be flat like colored paper cut-outs placed next to each other. To do this, Gustav used a little trick. A telescope makes things much bigger and draws them closer. But, at the same time, it makes them seem flat. Gustav then took a powerful telescope and often painted the houses and woods from the opposite bank, several miles away. Once you know this, it's easier to understand why his paintings look like colorfully woven carpets and have a fairy-tale quality about them.

Gustav loved flowers. Colorful blooms play an important role in his paintings. In his post-cards to Emilie he often wrote about flowers that he had seen or those that were about to come out.

He planted flowers outside his studio in Vienna and looked after them lovingly. When the famous artist Egon Schiele was young, he visited Gustav and wrote about the artist's studio: "It was in a garden — in one of those old, hidden gardens (...) — at the back of which there was a small, single-story house with lots of windows, shaded by tall trees. The way in was between flowers and ivy."

CHURCH AT UNTERACH ON LAKE ATTER

15

PORTRAIT OF SONJA KNIPS

AS PRETTY

As Gustav became well-known relatively early, many of the up-per-middle class lined up to have their portraits painted by him.

It was especially those in imperial Austria who had recently become rich, such as factory owners, bankers, and brewers, who were interested in the new style of painting. The royal court and the nobility on the other hand were not at all enthusiastic.

Gustav's portraits are almost all of women, dressed like princesses in expensive gowns. He painted faces and hands as carefully and as naturally as possible, while the materials of the clothes, furnishings, and carpets were turned into beauti-ful patterns. He even took this so far as to add real gold, silver, and glittering stones to his pictures next to the rich colors. It's no surprise that many of the women in the portraits — and, even more so, their husbands — felt particularly flattered.

PORTRAIT OF ADELE BLOCH-BAUER I

AS PRINCESSES

Now and again while he was painting their portraits, some of the women including Sonja Knips and Adele Bloch-Bauer fell in love with the artist, who was said to have had a particularly appealing personality. Sometimes Gustav Klimt even made little hints at these love affairs in his paintings. Sonja, for example, in the picture on the left, is shown holding one of the artist's small, red sketchbooks in her hand, which Gustav had given to her as a present. Adele's dress is covered with a decorative pattern in which the artist has played around with her initials, A and B. But there are also some other coded messages in his paintings which could only be understood by the lovers themselves.

17

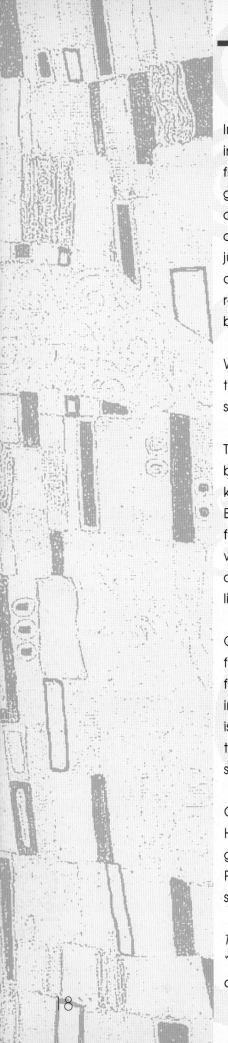
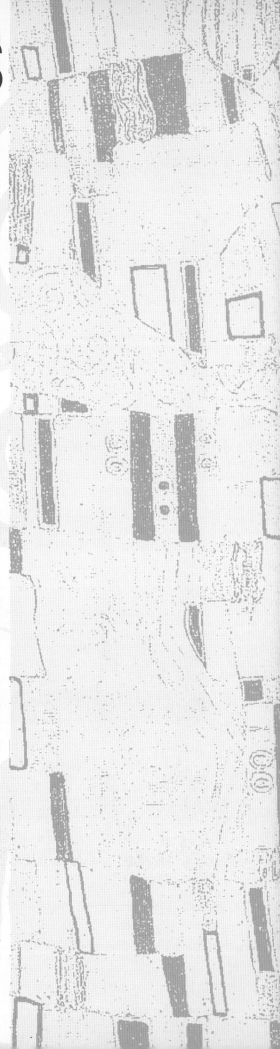

THE KISS

In 1908 Gustav Klimt completed his best-known painting of two lovers: *The Kiss.* Set in a brightly colored flower meadow, the embracing couple are clothed in golden robes. The young woman's eyes are closed and her head is tilted back, cradled in the man's arm, as she waits for his kiss. He is leaning towards her and is just about to kiss her. The couple seem to be in their own world, protected by a golden cocoon that surrounds them and sets them apart from the darker background. Its golden spirals stand for everlasting life.

While the man's gown is decorated largely with rectangular shapes, the woman's dress is covered with softer, rounded forms as well as a number of flowers.

The picture is quite clearly a celebration of the love between a man and a woman. For Gustav, hugs and kisses went hand in hand with happiness and harmony. But could it also be a painting to show the artist's love for Emilie? There is a lot that suggests it is. The laurel wreath on the man's head and his priest-like robe hint at an artist, and the woman's features look very much like Emilie's.

Gustav got the idea for many of his material patterns from Japanese art, and the gold in which he clad his figures was inspired by a visit to St. Apollinaire's church in Ravenna, Italy, and St. Mark's basilica in Venice. This is where he saw the golden mosaics on the walls and in the domes, which show emperors, empresses, and saints dressed in such luxurious, glittering gowns.

Gustav Klimt liked to use gold in his earlier works, too. He even decorated a whole dining room with a golden mosaic. This room is in the famous Stoclet Palace in Brussels, Belgium, where the highlight of the story told in pictures is also a couple kissing.

The Kiss of 1908 was to be the last painting of Gustav's "golden period." From then on, he simply used bright colors instead.

THE KISS

GUSTAV IN HIS ARTIST'S SMOCK

THE ARTIST'S LAST STUDIO

A DAY IN THE LIFE OF
GUSTAV KLIMT

GUSTAV KLIMT (3RD FROM LEFT) OUTSIDE THE CAFÉ IN TIVOLI GARDENS, VIENNA

SCHÖNBRUNN PARK

Gustav was an early riser. He was always up and about by 6 o'clock. He would then leave his flat, where he lived with his mother and his two sisters, and walked two-and-a-half miles to Tivoli Gardens on the edge of the grounds of Schönbrunn Palace, where he had his breakfast. On the way he passed a large pond with a statue of Neptune which he also painted once. Gustav liked to have a long breakfast, usually with friends of his. He often drank a whole bowlful of cream, which in those days was thought to help you keep strong and healthy. While having breakfast he used to read the newspapers. He then took a horse-drawn coach to his studio where he would try to work undisturbed the whole day long — not even taking a break for lunch. But now and again visitors dropped in, as did beggars to whom he was very generous, always giving them some money. In the evening Gustav ate at home or at a friend's house. He had a huge appetite, and it is known that he was always given two helpings! Sometimes he went to the theater or a concert, and Emilie frequently accompanied him. Or he would go and play skittles, a sport similar to bowling, which he was particularly fond of. Gustav was an easy-going man who liked to crack jokes and tease people in his thick Viennese accent — an accent which nobody could ever have mistaken.

WORK IN THE STUDIO

Gustav Klimt didn't like to be disturbed when he was painting, as he worked very long hours and concentrated hard on his pictures, which sometimes took months to complete. Every now and again he would work on several canvases at the same time, interrupting his work on one painting to continue on another one. After a longer break he would often see his work in a different light.

Gustav wore a long artist's smock which he became well known for. But because he didn't wash it very often it must have smelled pretty badly! He loved cats and there were always several in his studio. The artist used to invite young men and women to pose as models for him, and looking through the thousands of drawings that he made of these models and their movements he would get new ideas for his large paintings. A famous Viennese architect and designer, Josef Hoffmann, made a box out of dark stained oak for Gustav to keep all his paints and brushes in.

In a room next to his studio, Gustav had a collection of works of art from other cultures. He had a number of Japanese woodcuts, a Samurai warrior's coat of armor, Chinese scroll paintings and pieces of clothing, African figures, and much more in addition. These objects often gave him the inspiration for patterns for the clothes of the figures in his paintings or for the backgrounds, as can be clearly seen in the second portrait he painted of Adele Bloch-Bauer.

GUSTAV KLIMT AND THE YOUNG PAINTERS

WINDOWS (HOUSE FACADE)

Gustav Klimt was the first president of the Secession and remained one of its key figures, being the most famous artist in Vienna at that time. For this reason, he was well respected by his artist colleagues. And so he used his authority to help young artists who were setting out on their artistic careers. For example, he made it possible for Oskar Kokoschka — and one year later, for Egon Schiele — to show their works at major exhibitions, helping them on the road to fame. These young artists greatly admired Gustav and, in their early days, tried to copy his style. This shows clearly in some of Oskar Kokoschka's paintings, but he was soon to develop his own individual style. Although Gustav didn't really like Oskar's way of painting, he could see how talented he was and supported him very generously.

Gustav's friendship with Egon Schiele was much closer. Egon was a great fan of Gustav's and painted many of his pictures based on Gustav's work. Egon was thrilled when Gustav bought some of his drawings or swapped a work for one of his own. Gustav, for his part, was very impressed by Egon's skill at painting faces and capturing people's expressions. He even adopted Egon's boldly drawn lines, as can be seen in his painting *Forester's House*.

When Gustav Klimt died in 1918, Egon Schiele made two drawings of the great master's face as he lay on his hospital bed.

FORESTER'S HOUSE IN WEISSENBACH ON LAKE ATTER

Throughout his life and in a number of his paintings Gustav Klimt took a close look at some of life's most important questions: at love between a man and a woman, the course life takes from childhood, through youth, and into old age, and at the subject of death. Sickness and death in particular were subjects which often occupied his thoughts. When he was just twelve years old, his sister Annerl died; when he was thirty, his father and his brother, Ernst, passed away. His mother never got over her sadness, nor did Klara, one of his other sisters.

He was not spared the death of one of his own children either. Otto, the second son he had with one of his models, Mizzi Zimmermann, died when he was just a few months old. At that time he painted a picture called *Hope*, which shows these two extremes very clearly — the joy at the thought of a new-born child, and the threat of death. The young woman he painted was very pregnant but behind her, Gustav painted Death in the shape of a skull. In his late work *Death and Life*, blossoming life in all its variety is pictured opposite the lonely figure of Death, but perhaps the many crosses on Death's robe are meant to show that Heaven is waiting for us.

On February 6, 1918, Gustav Klimt died as the result of a stroke.

THE STOCLET FRIEZE (THE TREE OF LIFE)

DEATH AND LIFE

THE PICTURES IN THIS BOOK

Unless otherwise stated all paintings are by
Gustav Klimt

Cover:
Adele Bloch-Bauer I (detail), see page 17

Front endpapers:
Poppy Field (detail), 1907
Oil on canvas, 110 x 110 cm
Österreichische Galerie Belvedere, Vienna

Page 2
Theater in Taormina, 1886/88
Oil on plaster, *c.* 750 x 400 cm
Ceiling fresco above the north stairwell
in the Burg Theater, Vienna

*The Hofburg Actor Josef Lewinsky as Carlos
in Clavigo*, 1895
Oil on canvas, 60 x 44 cm
Österreichische Galerie Belvedere, Vienna

Page 3
Auditorium of the Burg Theater, 1888
Gouache on paper, 82 x 93 cm
Wien Museum, Vienna

Page 4
*First Exhibition of the Society of Pictorial Artists
in Austria – Secession*, 1898
Poster (lithograph), 62 x 43 cm
Wien Museum, Vienna

Page 5
Pallas Athena, 1898
Oil on canvas, 75 x 75 cm
Wien Museum, Vienna

Page 6
Medicine, 1901–07
Oil on canvas, 430 x 300 cm
Lost in a fire at Schloss Immendorf in 1945

Philosophy, 1899–1907
Oil on canvas, 430 x 300 cm
Lost in a fire at Schloss Immendorf in 1945

Jurisprudence, 1903–07
Oil on canvas, 430 x 300 cm
Lost in a fire at Schloss Immendorf in 1945

Page 7
Hygieia, detail from *Medicine*

Page 8
The Secession Building (designed by Joseph
Maria Olbrich), 1897–98
Photograph, *c.* 1900
Wien Museum, Vienna

The Hostile Powers
from the *Beethoven Frieze*, 1901/02
Casein paint on plaster, applications of stucco,
with glass, mother-of-pearl, and other materials,
incl. gold leaf, on mortar
(Here: detail of end wall, overall dimensions
217 x 639 cm)
Österreichische Galerie Belvedere, Vienna

Page 9
Here's a Kiss for all the World
from the *Beethoven Frieze*
(Here: detail of right-hand wall, overall
dimensions 217 x 1403 cm)
Österreichische Galerie Belvedere, Vienna

Page 10
Emilie Flöge in her fashion store in Vienna, 1910
Photograph by Madame d'Ora
Österreichische Galerie Belvedere, Vienna

Emilie Flöge Aged 17, 1891
Chalk on cardboard, 67 x 41.5 cm
Private collection

Page 11
Portrait of Emilie Flöge, 1902
Oil on canvas, 181 x 84 cm
Wien Museum, Vienna

Page 12
Gustav Klimt and Emilie Flöge in a rowboat
near the mooring at Villa Paulick
Photograph, 1909
Private collection

Letter from Gustav Klimt to Maria Zimmermann
with an explanatory sketch of his "viewfinder"
Klimt-Archiv, Albertina, Vienna

Page 13
A Farmhouse on Lake Atter, 1914
Oil on canvas, 110 x 110 cm
Private collection

Page 14
Gustav Klimt with a telescope on the landing
stage at Villa Paulick in Seewäldchen, 1904
Photograph, 1904
Private collection

Gustav Klimt in the garden of his studio in
Josefstädterstrasse 21, Vienna VIII, *c.* 1910
Photograph by Moriz Nähr
Österreichische Nationalbibliothek, Bildarchiv,
Vienna

Page 15
Church at Unterach on Lake Atter, 1916
Oil on canvas, 110 x 110 cm
Private collection

Page 16
Portrait of Sonja Knips, 1898
Oil on canvas, 141 x 141 cm
Österreichische Galerie Belvedere,
Vienna

Page 17
Portrait of Adele Bloch-Bauer I, 1907
Oil, silver, and gold leaf, 138 x 138 cm
Neue Galerie, New York

Page 19
The Kiss, 1907/08
Oil on canvas, 180 x 180 cm
Österreichische Galerie Belvedere,
Vienna

Page 20
Gustav Klimt in his artist's smock, holding
a cat outside his studio, *c.* 1912–14
Photograph by Moriz Nähr
Österreichische Nationalbibliothek, Bildarchiv,
Vienna

Gustav Klimt's studio in Feldmühlgasse 11,
Vienna VIII, photographed in 1918 shortly
after his death, showing the last paintings he
was working on
Österreichische Nationalbibliothek, Bildarchiv,
Vienna

Gustav Klimt outside the café in Tivoli Gardens,
near Schönbrunn
Photograph, *c.* 1914
Österreichische Nationalbibliothek, Bildarchiv,
Vienna